THEN AND NOW

COMMUNITY HELPERS

Bobbie Kalman

Go to
www.openlightbox.com
and enter this book's
unique code.

ACCESS CODE

LBXY2772

Lightbox is an all-inclusive digital solution for the teaching and learning of curriculum topics in an original, groundbreaking way. Lightbox is based on National Curriculum Standards.

LIGHTBOX SUPPLEMENTARY RESOURCES

SHARE
Share titles within your Learning Management System (LMS) or Library Circulation System

CURRICULUM
Find national and state curriculum correlations

CITATION
Create bibliographical references following the Chicago Manual of Style

STANDARD FEATURES OF LIGHTBOX

AUDIO High-quality narration using text-to-speech system

ACTIVITIES Printable PDFs that can be emailed and graded

SLIDESHOWS Pictorial overviews of key concepts

VIDEOS Embedded high-definition video clips

WEBLINKS Curated links to external, child-safe resources

TRANSPARENCIES Step-by-step layering of maps, diagrams, charts, and timelines

INTERACTIVE MAPS Interactive maps and aerial satellite imagery

QUIZZES Ten multiple-choice questions that are automatically graded and emailed for teacher assessment

KEY WORDS Matching key concepts to their definitions

Lightbox Grades 3–5 Subscription
ISBN 978-1-5105-5424-5

Access hundreds of Lightbox titles with our digital subscription. Sign up for a **FREE** subscription trial at **www.openlightbox.com/trial**

THEN AND NOW

COMMUNITY HELPERS

Contents

Community Helpers

A community is a place where many people live and work together and share buildings, **services**, and laws. Community helpers are people who make communities cleaner, safer, and better.

Community helpers work in many professional fields, including healthcare.

Community Helpers Long Ago

In the past, there were not as many kinds of community helpers as there are today. Some helpers, such as store owners, supplied people with important things they needed. Some drove wagons. Community helpers called tradespeople were very important because they made things that people needed.

Wagon drivers helped people in different ways. For instance, some transported goods, while others delivered mail.

Tradespeople Long Ago

Before there were modern machines, tradespeople made everything by hand using simple tools. Carpenters, wheelwrights, harness makers, and blacksmiths were some tradespeople in old communities.

Trade Jobs

Tradespeople in the past helped produce many different objects using various materials.

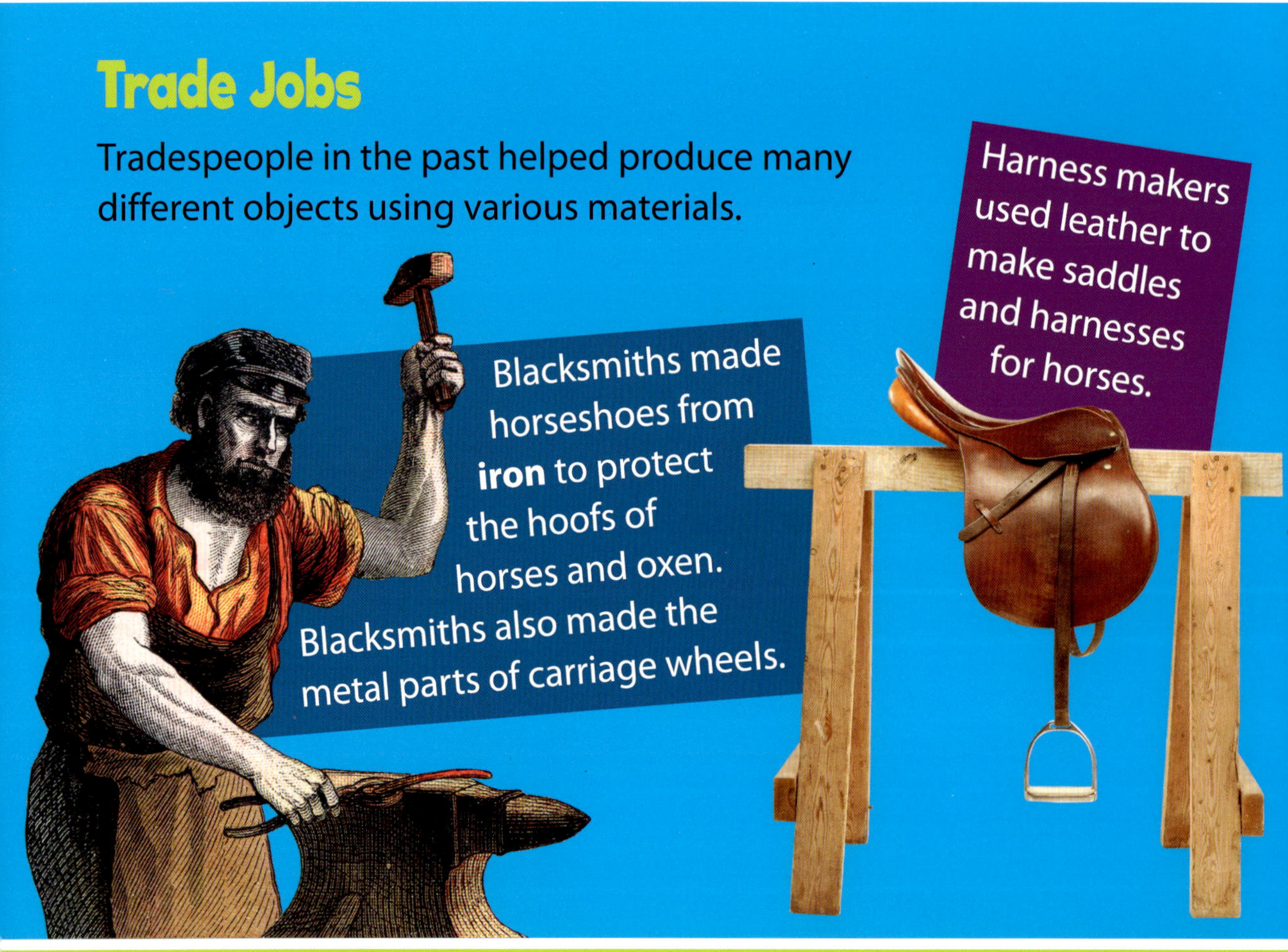

Harness makers used leather to make saddles and harnesses for horses.

Blacksmiths made horseshoes from **iron** to protect the hoofs of horses and oxen. Blacksmiths also made the metal parts of carriage wheels.

In the past, tradespeople used tools that did not require electricity to work.

Wheelwrights made wagon wheels from wood and iron.

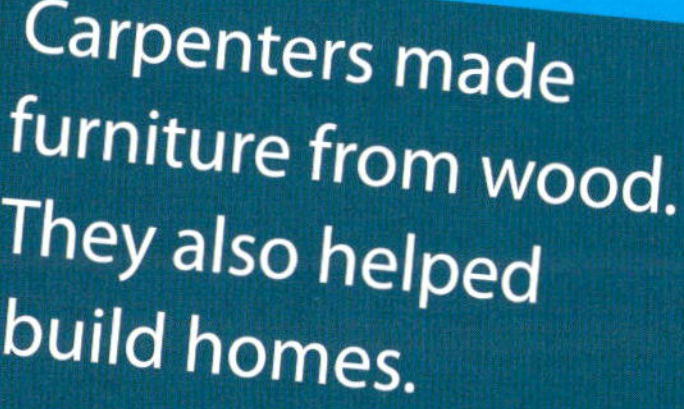

Carpenters made furniture from wood. They also helped build homes.

Tradespeople Today

Tradespeople today are still important community helpers. What they make and how they do it may be very different from how tradespeople did it long ago. In the past, for example, wainwrights, or wagon-repair workers, fixed wagons, while today, **mechanics** fix cars. Tradespeople today still use some simple tools, but they also use new kinds of machines to do their work.

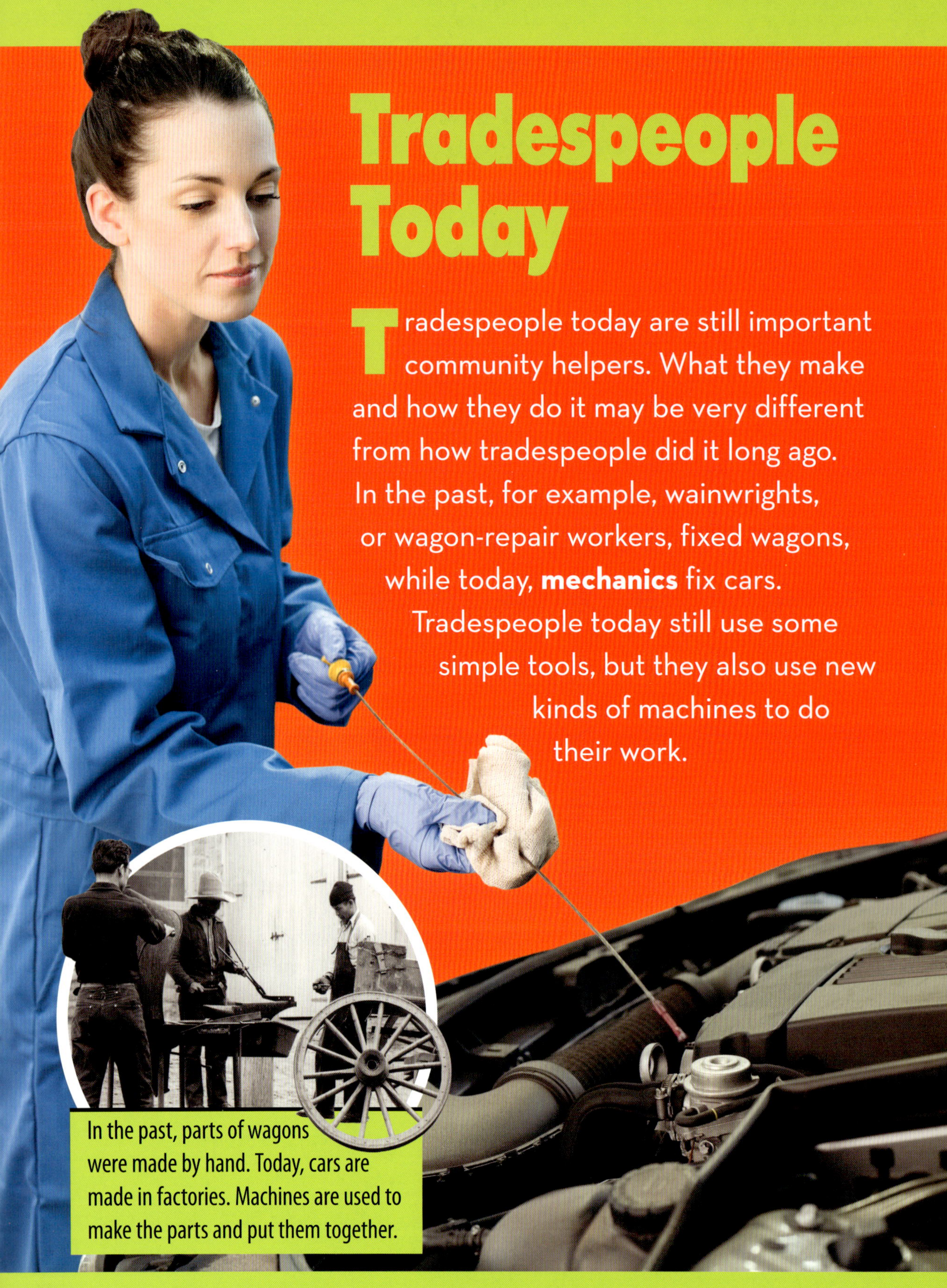

In the past, parts of wagons were made by hand. Today, cars are made in factories. Machines are used to make the parts and put them together.

Community Helpers Timeline

Community helpers have always been important around the world. They kept their communities safe and provided them with important tools and objects.

1500 BC — The Hittites, ancient inhabitants of the area now known as Türkiye, become the first blacksmiths by discovering how to forge iron.

6 AD — In the ancient city of Rome, Emperor Augustus creates a team called the Vigiles to fight fires with buckets and pumps.

1850s — Full-time firefighters begin working in the United States.

1854 — British **nurse** Florence Nightingale establishes the modern profession of nursing by creating a military hospital for British soldiers.

1887–1889 — The Eiffel Tower is built in Paris, France. About 150 blacksmiths forge 18,000 iron pieces, and between 150 and 300 construction workers assemble them to build the monument.

2020–2022 — The COVID-19 pandemic develops around the world. Almost 1 million U.S. healthcare professionals contract the virus while working on the front lines.

Construction Workers

Construction workers are tradespeople who build homes, offices, schools, hospitals, and many other buildings. They also build roads and bridges. They use many kinds of tools and machines, including power drills, cranes, bulldozers, and cement trucks.

The construction workers of the past did not wear personal protective equipment. Today, construction workers wear different kinds of safety gear to protect themselves.

Builders in the Past

Long ago, there were very few machines, so builders used simple tools, such as hammers, saws, and axes. It took a long time to construct a building. After more machines were invented, tall buildings could be built quickly.

Construction Workers in the United States: 1940–2020

In your opinion, what could be the reasons for the changes in the number of U.S. construction workers over time?

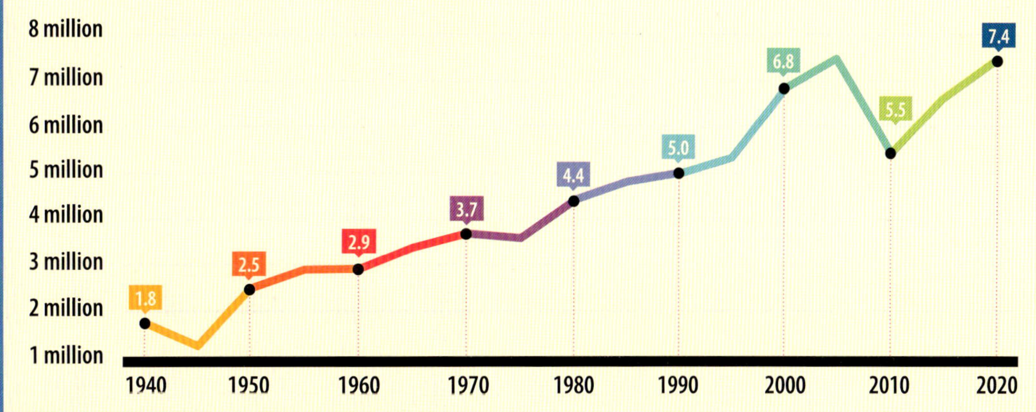

Crossing guards help children reach school safely. Some of them are volunteers, while others are paid workers.

School Helpers

Most of the people who work at your school are teachers, but some school workers help you in other ways. The principal is the head of the school. The librarian shows you how to find the books you need.

Who Were the Helpers?

Long ago, many schools had only one room and one teacher. Not only did teachers plan lessons and teach their students, they also had to keep the school clean. Students helped them sweep the floor, wash the blackboard, and bring in water from the well. The parents of the students paid the teacher's **salary**.

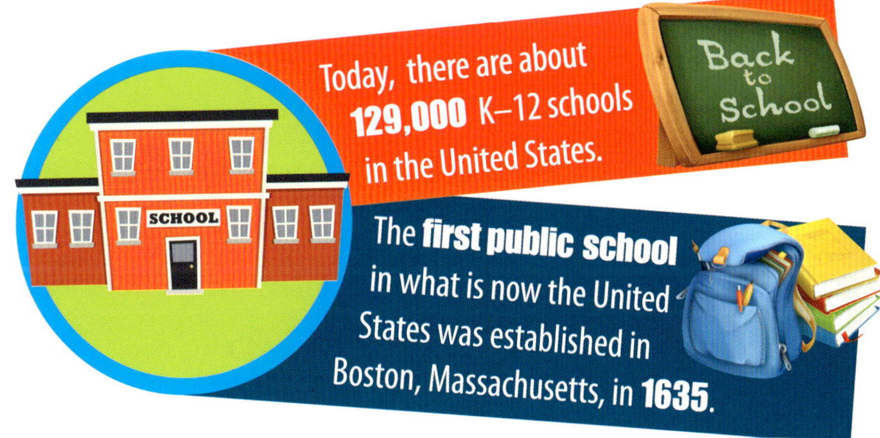

Food and Farm Workers

Next to air and water, food is the most important thing we need to stay alive. **Agricultural** workers, or farmers, grow the food we eat. Farms send some of this food to factories, where it can be made into different kinds of foods. These foods are then sold in supermarkets. Many people help get food from farms to our tables.

Are You a Helper?

Do you have a garden at home? If so, how do you help care for it? Do you help your parents with grocery shopping or cooking? What can you cook?

Farming Long Ago

In the past, most people got their food from gardens they planted next to their homes. People also raised chickens, pigs, and one or two horses and cows. Farmers in the past typically had large fields where they grew corn or wheat. Farm helpers were often family members, including children.

In 2021, U.S. farmers produced more than 1.3 million tons (1.2 million metric tons) of strawberries.

U.S. FARMING TODAY

The United States has more than 2 MILLION farms.

Texas has more farms than any other state, with about 247,000.

Approximately 895 MILLION acres (362 million hectares) of U.S. land is used for farming.

98 PERCENT of U.S. farms are family businesses.

Medical Helpers

Medical helpers are nurses, dentists, and many kinds of doctors who treat different body parts, such as eyes or teeth. The pharmacist at your drugstore is another important helper because he or she gives you the medicine you need to get well.

Medical Helpers Long Ago

In the old days, the same doctor that treated your illnesses also looked after your teeth and your eyes. He often traveled from one small community to another to help sick people. In those days, people did not know that **germs** caused many **diseases**. In fact, they thought that taking too many baths could make them sick! Doctors often passed along diseases because they did not wash their hands or the instruments, or tools, they used.

Modern-day dentists use different types of tools. They make sure that these tools are always properly cleaned before using them on patients.

What Do You Think?

Today, medical professionals wear gloves and a face masks. What other measures do they take to keep their patients safe?

First Responders

First responders are emergency workers who are the first to respond, or act, in emergencies. An emergency is a dangerous situation that happens suddenly. First responders include police officers, ambulance drivers, paramedics, and firefighters. In emergencies, **operators** receive calls from people who need help. They then send emergency workers to where they are needed.

No Emergency Help

In the past, there were no telephones or emergency numbers to call. There were no first responders, either. When there was an emergency, people helped one another. In big cities, there were hospitals, but their ambulances were horse-drawn wagons.

The ambulance service of Bellevue Hospital, in New York City, New York, was first established in 1869. It was one of the first ambulance services in the United States.

First Responders Map

Emergencies happen all around the world. Every country has a different system in place for people to seek help in an emergency.

United States

People in the United States can call 911 for every type of emergency. For this reason, 911 is known as a "universal emergency number."

Italy

The Italian universal emergency number is 112. However, people in Italy can also use different numbers for specific emergencies. They can call 113 for police, 118 for paramedics, and 115 for firefighters.

Japan

Japan has two different emergency numbers. For medical problems or in case of fire, Japanese people call 119. For criminal activities and accidents, they can reach the police by calling 110.

Firefighters

Fires can start quickly. Firefighters help fight fires and rescue people and animals. They put out fires that start in buildings. They also fight forest and bush fires. Firefighters today drive big trucks and use water from **fire hydrants** to put out fires. Fire hydrants can be found in many places around towns and cities.

Some modern fire departments have fire engines equipped with tanks that can contain more than 4,000 gallons (15,100 liters) of water.

Many Fires

Long ago, people used candles for light and fireplaces for cooking and to heat homes. Open flames made accidental fires very common. In those days, there were no fire trucks or firefighters, so buckets of water were used to put out fires. Later, firefighters drove fire trucks with pumps, which sprayed water on fires.

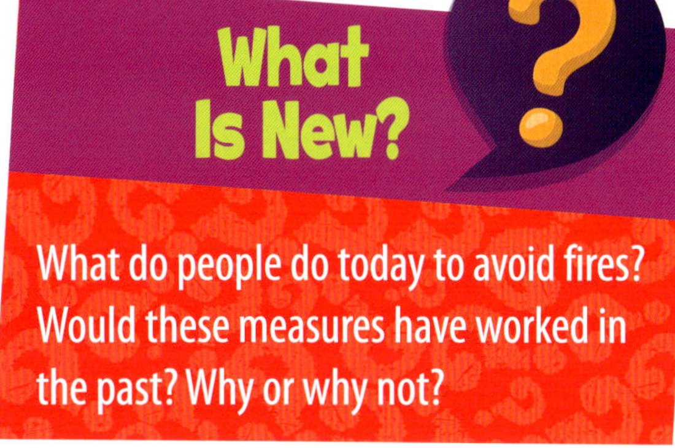

What Is New?

What do people do today to avoid fires? Would these measures have worked in the past? Why or why not?

Before modern fire engines were invented, early fire trucks were pulled by horses.

In the past, buckets of water were passed along lines of people to put out the flames of a fire.

Today, firefighters use fire engines and other different vehicles. They even use helicopters to drop buckets of water on forest or bush fires.

Quiz

1 Who created the Vigiles in Ancient Rome?

2 What pulled early fire trucks?

3 What numbers should be called for emergencies in Japan?

4 From where did most people get their food in the past?

5 How many metal pieces were used to build the Eiffel Tower?

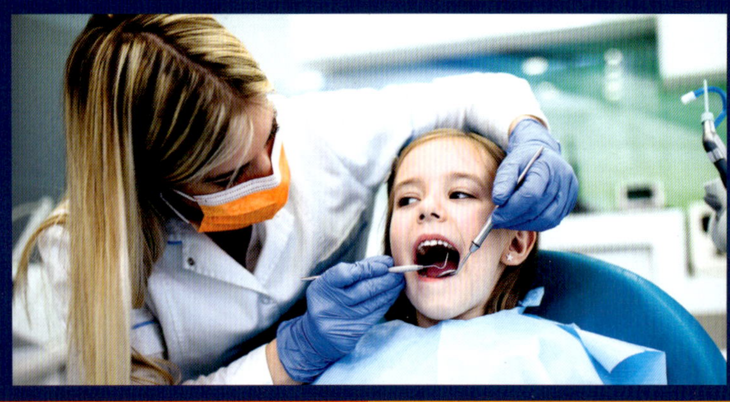

6 When did full-time firefighters begin working in United States?

7 Why were fires more frequent in the past?

8 How many K–12 are there in the United States today?

ANSWERS

1. Emperor Augustus **2.** Horses **3.** 119 for medical problems or in case of fire, 110 to reach the police **4.** From gardens they planted next to their homes and from animals they raised **5.** 18,000 **6.** In the 1850s **7.** Open flames in candles and fireplaces made accidental fires very common. **8.** About 129,000

Key Words

agricultural: related to growing crops and raising livestock

diseases: conditions in a person's body that make the person sick

fire hydrant: a covered pipe connected to water where hoses can be attached

germs: tiny organisms that can cause diseases

iron: a grayish-white metal used for making horseshoes and other things

mechanics: people whose job is repairing vehicles or other kinds of machines

nurse: a person trained to care for sick or injured people

operators: people who operate a piece of equipment, machine, or telephone

salary: money paid to a person regularly for doing a job

services: jobs or helpful acts

Index

SUPPLEMENTARY RESOURCES

Click on the plus icon found in the bottom left corner of each spread to open additional teacher resources.

- Download and print the book's quizzes and activities
- Access curriculum correlations
- Explore additional web applications that enhance the Lightbox experience

LIGHTBOX DIGITAL TITLES
Packed full of integrated media

VIDEOS

INTERACTIVE MAPS

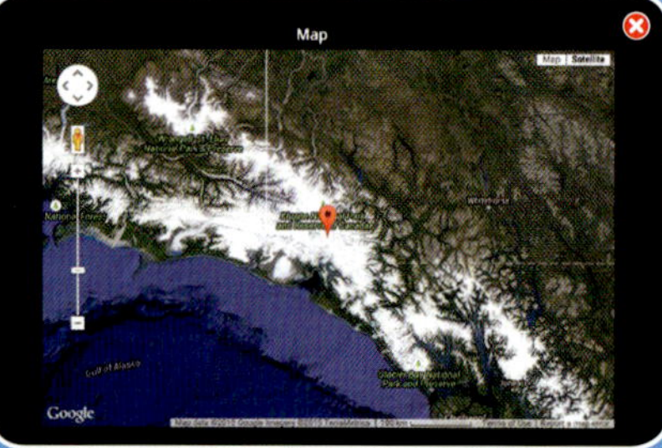

WEBLINKS

SLIDESHOWS

QUIZZES

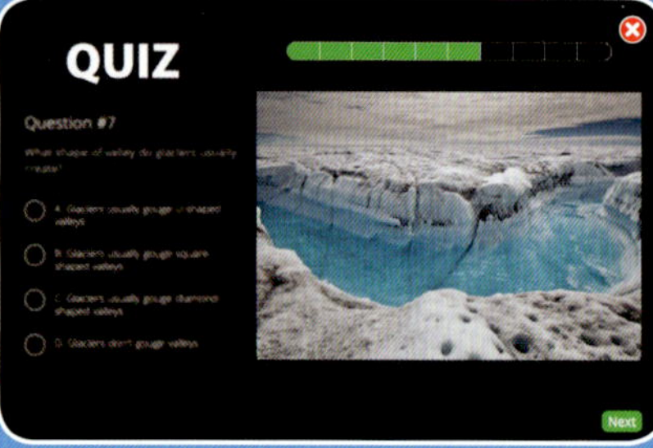

OPTIMIZED FOR

- ✓ TABLETS
- ✓ WHITEBOARDS
- ✓ COMPUTERS
- ✓ AND MUCH MORE!

Published by Lightbox Learning Inc.
276 5th Avenue, Suite 704 #917
New York, NY 10001
Website: www.openlightbox.com

First published by Crabtree Publishing Company in 2014

Library of Congress Control Number: 2020942100

ISBN 978-1-5105-5494-8 (hardcover)
ISBN 978-1-5105-5495-5 (multi-user eBook)

Printed in Guangzhou, China
1 2 3 4 5 6 7 8 9 0 26 25 24 23 22

082022
111021

Photo Credits
Every reasonable effort has been made to trace ownership and to obtain permission to reprint copyright material. The publisher would be pleased to have any errors or omissions brought to its attention so that they may be corrected in subsequent printings. The publisher acknowledges Alamy, Getty Images, Shutterstock, and Bridgeman Images as its primary image suppliers for this title.

Project Coordinator Sara Cucini
Designer Ana María Vidal